BY LOUISE GUHL

Contents

UNIT 1.................................. 3
  Triplets

UNIT 2.................................. 11
  Playing With Two Hands On Both Staffs

UNIT 3.................................. 18
  Fingering Legato Phrases

UNIT 4.................................. 23
  Bass Clef On Both Staffs

UNIT 5.................................. 31
  Treble Clef On Both Staffs

UNIT 6.................................. 39
  A New Way To Count

ISBN 0-8497-7429-3

© **1990 Neil A. Kjos Music Company**, 4380 Jutland Drive, San Diego, California 92117. International copyright secured. All rights reserved. Printed in U.S.A.
WARNING! All the music and text in this book are protected by copyright law. To copy or reproduce them by any method is an infringement of the copyright law. Anyone who reproduces copyrighted matter is subject to substantial penalties and assessments for each infringement.

Preface to Teachers

The Magic Reader, Book 4 continues the process developed in **The Magic Readers, Books 1–3**.

There are six units, each addressing a specific reading requirement.
1. counting triplets
2. playing notes on the lower or upper staff with both hands
3. legato fingering in the range wider than five keys
4. both staffs with bass clef
5. both staffs with treble clef
6. $\frac{6}{8}$ meter and legato pedal

Each unit presents a new concept, three to seven pages of short musical pieces to read, and technical exercises to develop physical ease with keyboard shapes that occur frequently in piano music.

The student continues to read music with either no key signature or a key signature with one sharp or one flat.

About the Author

Louise Guhl's fascination with how students learn led to the development of **The Magic Reader** series. She is an independent piano teacher in Dassel, Minnesota, who is also popular as a clinician. In the past she has taught pedagogy and class piano at the University of Minnesota, the McPhail School of Music, and Concordia College (St. Paul).

After graduation from St. Olaf College she studied in Berlin, Germany. Mrs. Guhl has also been a piano student of Guy Maier and Bernhard Weiser, and a pedagogy student of Guy Duckworth. She is the author of *Keyboard Proficiency* for college students.

UNIT 1

Triplets

Challenge

To learn to count three eighth notes in the same time a quarter note lasts.

To Get Ready

1. Walk and count aloud one beat for each step.

2. Walk and say these three syllables for each step.

              1 - and - a   2 - and - a   3 - and - a   4 - and - a

When you or your teacher write the counting in your book, you'll probably want to write it 1 + a   2 + a.

3. As you walk, count and clap, or play rhythm sticks, three times for each step.

You have been playing triplets.

Triplets look like this.

The slur under the notes does *not* tell you to play legato. The slur and the italic *3* tell you to play a triplet.

Notice the difference between the *3* that tells you to play a triplet, and the 3 that tells you to play your third finger.

Remember

A triplet lasts as long as two eighth notes.

WP318

Read

8va - - - - - - - - - - - - - - - - - above the staff means to play an octave higher

ff (fortissimo) tells you to play louder than *forte* (*f*).

pp (pianissimo) tells you to play softer than *piano* (*p*).

rit. the abbreviation for *ritardando*, tells you to count gradually slower.

NEAR AND FAR AWAY

⌢ This sign is called a fermata. It tells you to allow the sound to last as long as you wish.

8va - - - - - - - - - - - - - ┘ below the staff tells you to play an octave lower.

PICCOLO AND BASSOON DUET

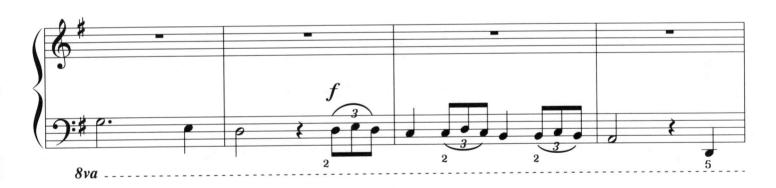
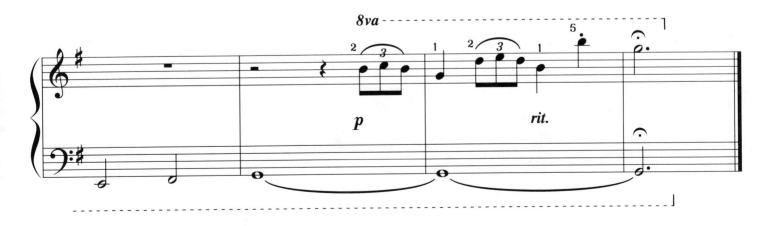

WP318

A WALK WITH A GRASSHOPPER

mf (mezzo forte) tells you to play softer than *f*, but louder than *p*.

SOLEMN MARCH

WP318

———————— tells you to gradually play more softly.

Allegretto tells you to play faster than Moderato, but not as fast as Allegro.

> is an accent mark, telling you to play that note louder.

MAKING A CHAIN

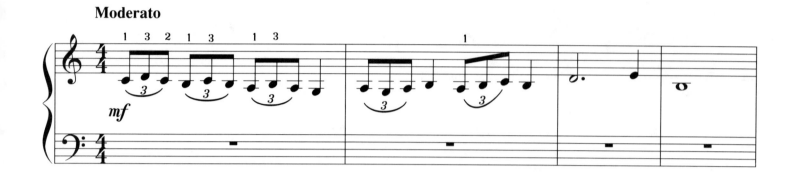
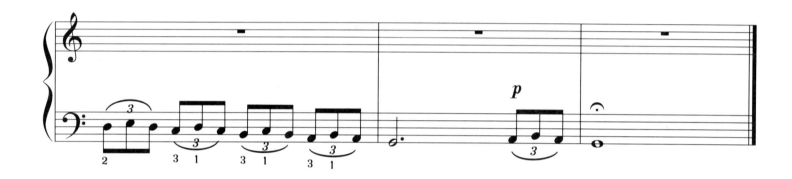

GOT STUCK!

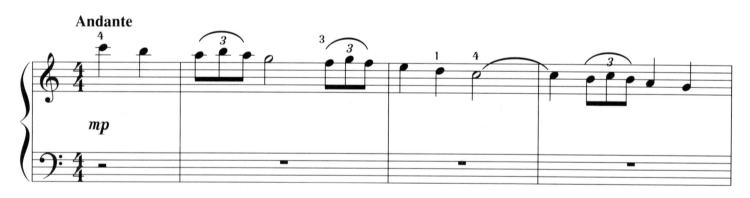

Technique

These exercises will help you learn to count while you play triplets. Be sure to count aloud!

1. Play first with fingers 1-4.
   Repeat with fingers 2-5.

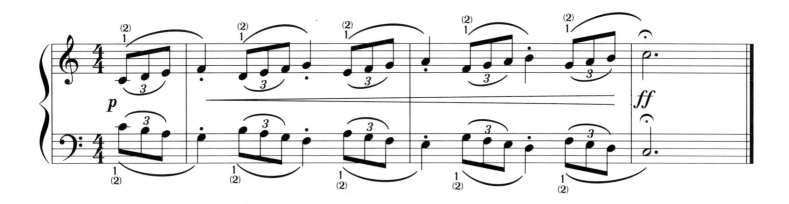

2. Continue the pattern up the keyboard until your thumbs reach C.

WP318

Play each exercise four times. Start *p*, increase to *mp*, then *mf*, then *f*.

UNIT 2

Playing With Two Hands On Both Staffs

Challenge

To play with the right hand on the bottom staff and the left hand on the top staff.

To Get Ready

Study these examples to learn how stems are placed on notes:

1. Stems go up on the right side of the note when the note is on the third line of the staff or lower.

2. Stems go down on the left side of the note when the note is on the third line or higher.

Place stems correctly on the notes on the grand staff below:

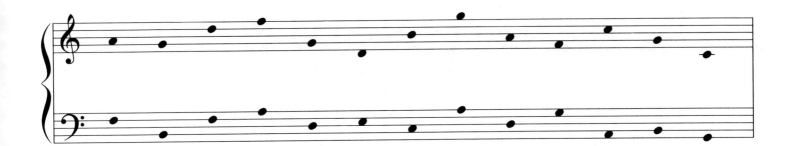

WP318

Now you know how stems are placed when all notes on the top staff are for the right hand, and all notes on the bottom staff are for the left hand. Sometimes you may have to play with both hands in the same staff!

When that happens, play the notes with the stems up with your right hand. Play notes with stems down with your left hand. Finger numbers for the Right Hand will be above the notes; for the Left Hand they will be below the notes.

Read

HOP SCOTCH IS TOP NOTCH

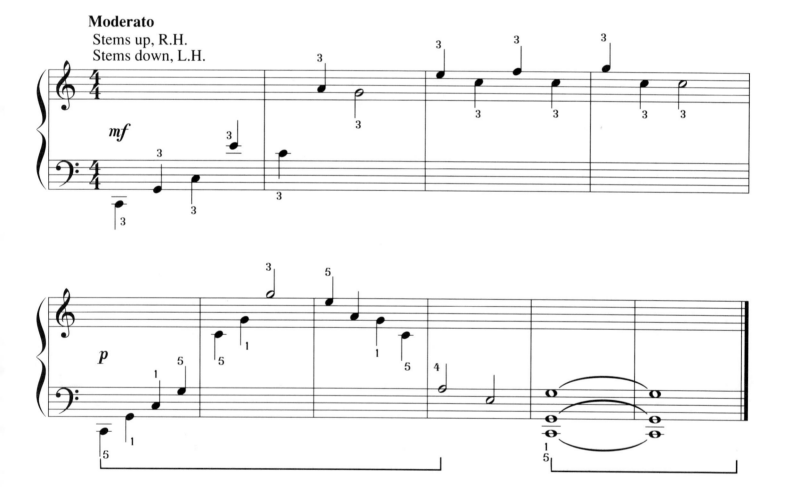

PING-PONG® PIZZAZZ

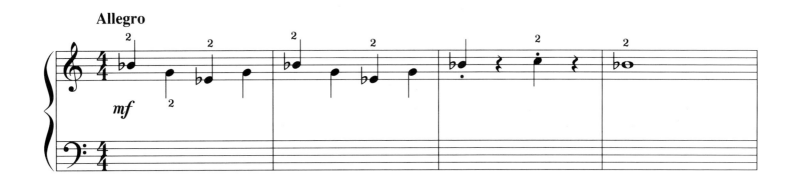

I WAS SCARED — BUT IT TURNED OUT O.K.

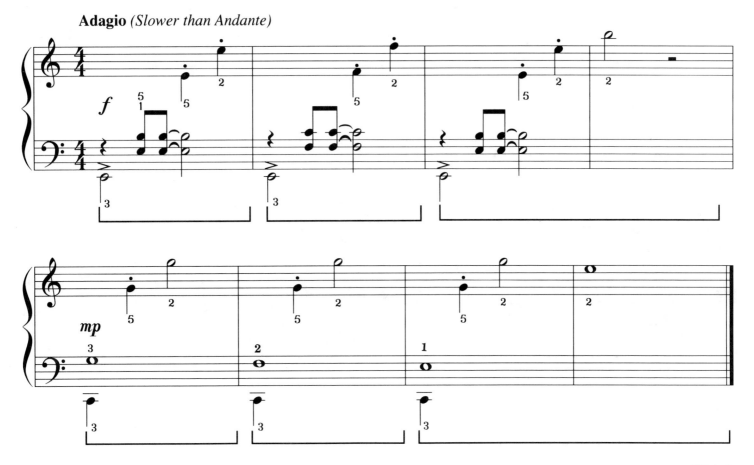

WAKE UP! IT'S A SUNNY DAY!

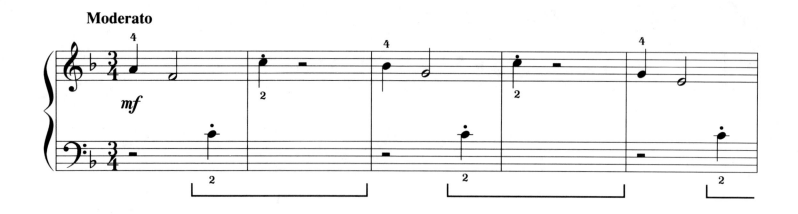
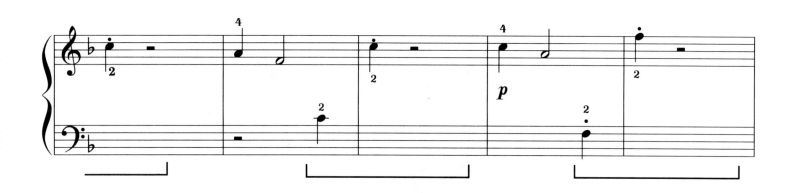
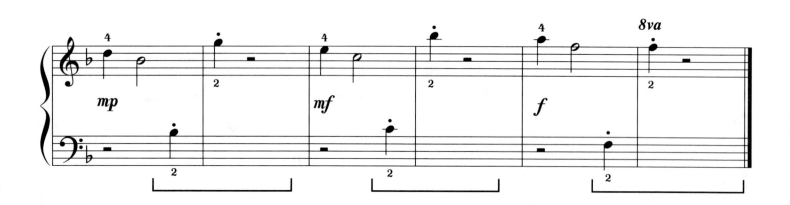

Play these pieces with the pedal. Use it any way you like.

When a pattern of triplets has been started, the triplet sign, 3, is often not used again.

HOW BIG I SOUND!

Technique

1. The notes below make an arpeggio (up and down) in the key of C on the I chord.

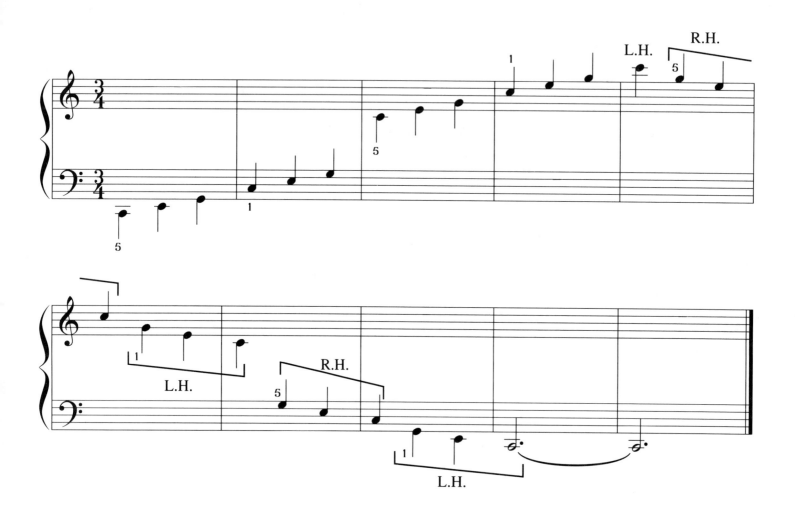

Practice the arpeggios on IV and V in the key of C. (For a review of these chords, see *The Magic Reader, Book 3* page 31, or ask your teacher.)

Practice the I, IV, and V arpeggios in the key of G the same way.

Now practice in the key of F.

2. Play the C scale "out" (up) in quarter notes, and come "in" (down) with eighth notes.

This is the C scale for three octaves. Play with your right hand.

Play the left hand down three octaves in quarter notes.

Start at this C.

Play back up four octaves in eighth notes. Start at this C:

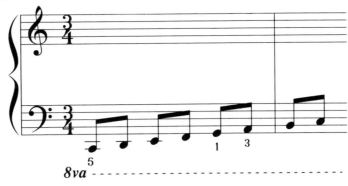

Practice G and F scales the same way.

Remember that the fingering for the F scale is different because of the location of the black key.

WP318

UNIT 3

Fingering Legato Phrases

Challenge

To notice finger numbers that help you play legato when the phrase extends beyond five notes.

To Get Ready

Study these examples from "Polly Put the Kettle On."

Right Hand: The 2-1 in the second measure tells you to stretch and skip a key.

The 1-5 makes your hand ready to reach the low notes.

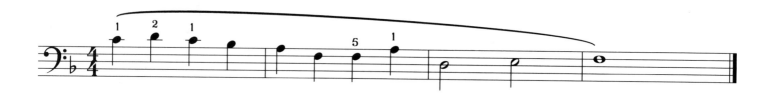

Left Hand: The 1-2-1 helps you have a finger for the highest key in the phrase, and then enough fingers to get down five keys.

The 5-1 makes your hand ready to reach the low note.

Remember

When the phrase extends beyond five notes, the fingering will be irregular. The finger numbers tell when to cross, stretch, or contract.

WP318

2. Add fingerings to the following examples so that the next time you play it will be easier. Always use pencil to write in fingerings because you may think of a better fingering the next time you play it.

Let the clef sign help you decide which hand will play.

Imagine how your fingers will feel on the keys
OR
Sight-read to find the problems.

There may be more than one way to finger well — choose the one that feels best for you.

American

WHERE, OH WHERE HAS MY LITTLE DOG GONE!

Traditional

THE MOCKING BIRD

American

LITTLE BROWN JUG

American

GOOD-BYE, OLD PAINT

American

SHE'LL BE COMIN' ROUND THE MOUNTAIN

American

FOR HE'S A JOLLY GOOD FELLOW

English

THE BLUE BELLS OF SCOTLAND

Scottish

Technique

These exercises will help you feel comfortable when you need to skip one key between the first and second fingers.

Practice each exercise, starting on each white key until you have played up or down one octave from where you started.

1.

2.

3.

4.

These exercises will help you skip two keys between the first and third fingers.

1.

2.

3.

4.

Another Scale to Practice
Play G scale the way you played C scale on page 15.

WP318

UNIT 4

Bass Clef On Both Staffs

Challenge

To play bass clef notes in both hands (so the staff for the Right Hand will be bass clef!).

To Get Ready

Play Number 1 with your right hand. Draw the bass clef sign in Number 1.

As you look at the top staff, play the notes you copied with your Right Hand. Write the correct fingering above the first note.

1.

Draw the bass clef sign at the beginning of the top staff of Number 2. Copy the notes and fingering you drew in the top staff of Number 1. Play hands together.

2.

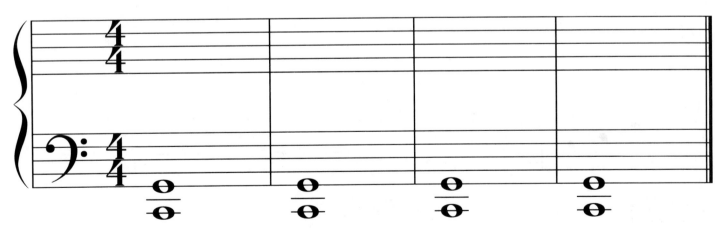

WP318

This is a duet. Your teacher will play the other part with you. Your teacher's part is on the next page. Both you and your teacher will have to count carefully to stay with each other! Your part says Secondo because you are playing the low part. Your teacher's part is called Primo because it is the high part.

Look to see if both hands play the same notes just one octave apart.

Since the notes on the upper staff are easier to read than the ledger notes on the lower staff, keep your eyes on the top staff and play the left hand one octave lower.

SHARING THE BENCH

Adolph Ruthardt

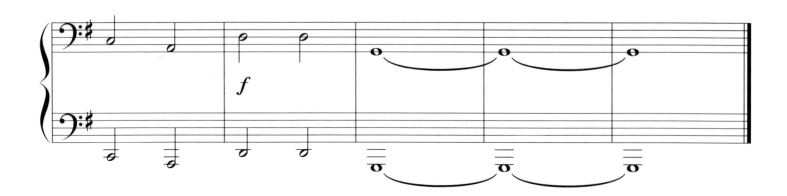

WP318

SHARING THE BENCH

Adolph Ruthardt

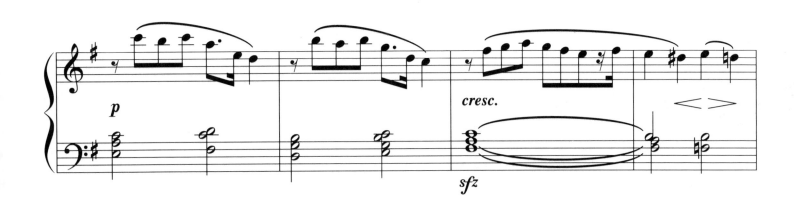

YANKEE DOODLE

American

MICHAEL, ROW THE BOAT ASHORE

Spiritual

WP318

AURA LEE

American

ELEPHANTS ON THE PROWL

Hold the last RH note as written, then quickly turn the page with your RH as your LH continues to play without stopping.

Adagio

WP318

LOOKING FOR SOMETHING IN THE BASEMENT

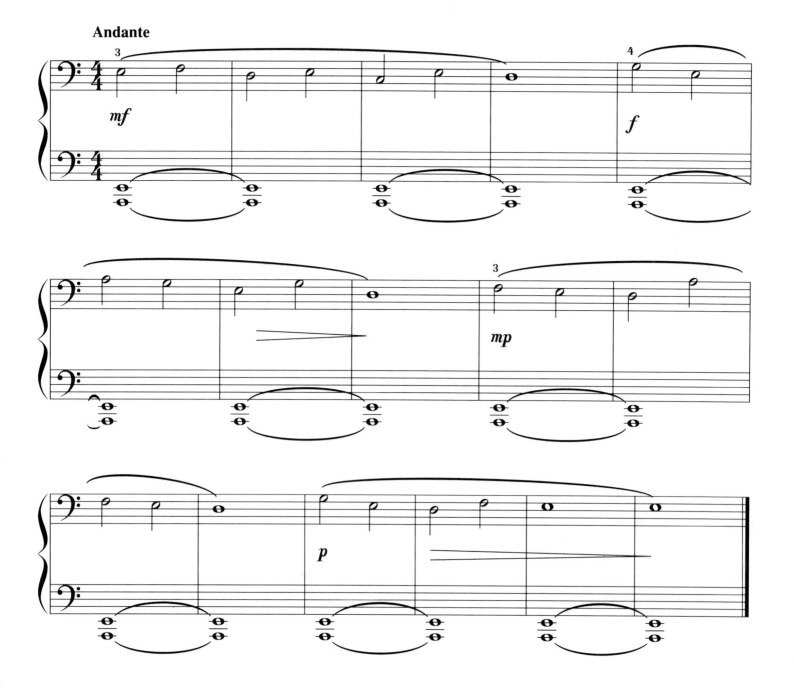

WP318

Technique

Inverting a triad upward. That means tipping it over, so the lowest key becomes the highest.

After you have played Number 1 looking at the notes, play it again and watch your fingers.

Describe how your fingers move from the root position to the first inversion.

Practice playing this with your eyes closed!

1. **Legato**

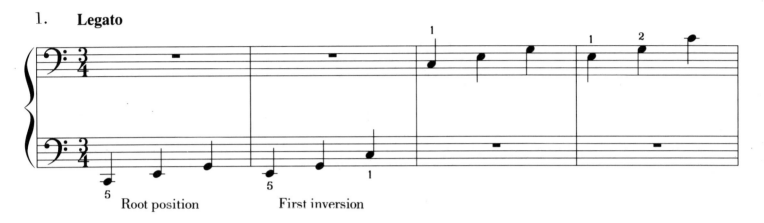

Practice Number 2 the way you practiced Number 1. You will play from the first inversion to root position.

2. **Legato**

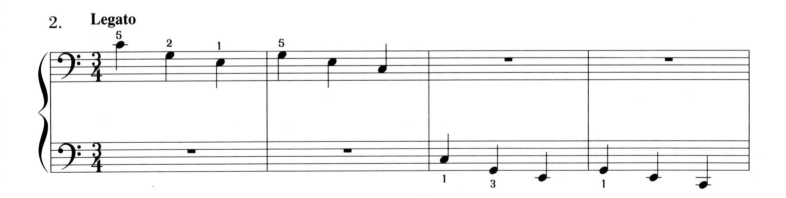

Practice inverting the F and G triads the same way in several different octaves.

3. Practice the first inversion arpeggios the way you practiced the root position on page 16.

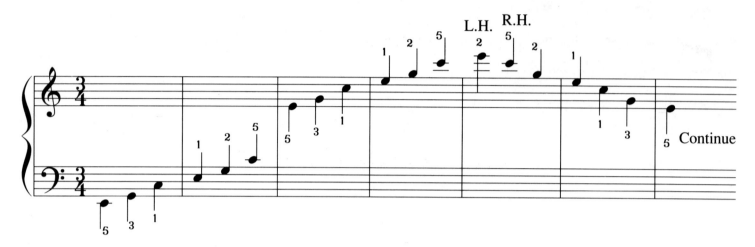

Draw the notes for the first inversion of the F triad.

Write in the fingering for the inversion for each hand.

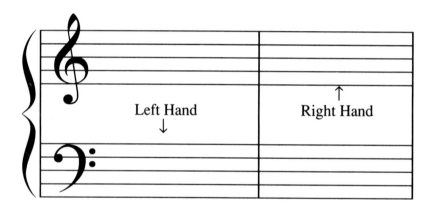

Draw the notes for the first inversion of the G triad.

Write in the fingering for the inversion for each hand.

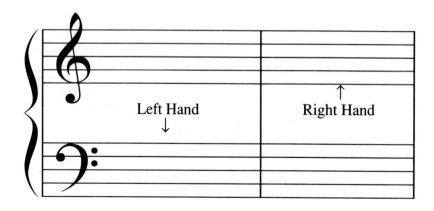

WP318

UNIT 5

Treble Clef On Both Staffs

Challenge

To play treble clef notes printed on the bottom staff with your left hand.

To Get Ready

Play Number 1 with your Left Hand.

Draw a treble clef sign in the bottom staff of Number 1.

Copy the notes in the top staff on the lower staff.

Look at the notes you wrote on the bottom staff and play your left hand.

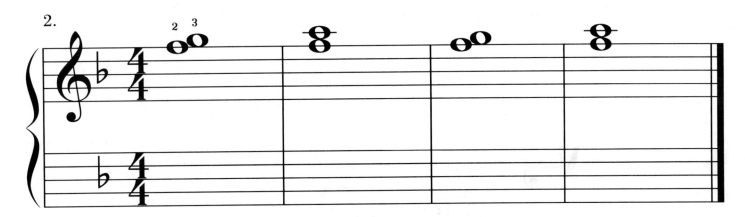

Draw a treble clef sign on the bottom staff of Number 2.

Copy the notes in the top staff of Number 1 on the bottom staff of Number 2. Write the correct fingering under the first note.

Play hands together.

WP318

SHE'LL BE COMIN' ROUND THE MOUNTAIN

American

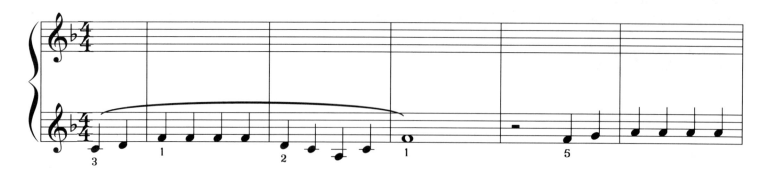

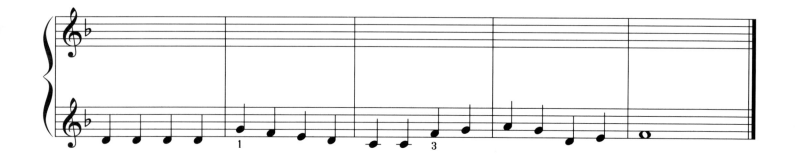

LAZY MARY, WILL YOU GET UP?

Nursery Tune

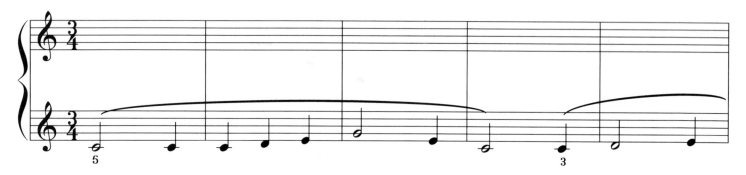

WP318

TEN LITTLE INDIANS

American

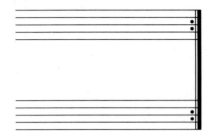

Repeat dots tell you to go back to the beginning and play again.

PRAISE TO THE LORD

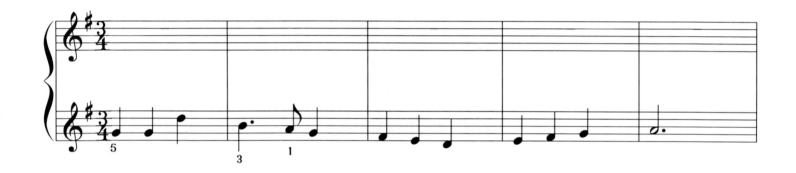

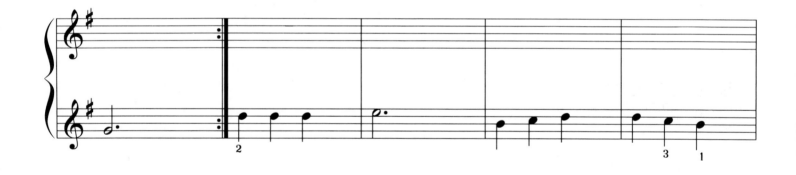

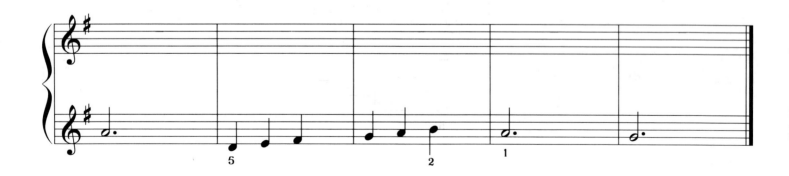

SKIP TO MY LOU

American

WIND BELLS

Hold the pedal down all the way through the piece.

WP318

MINKA

This is your part.

Russian Folk Song
arr. Adolph Ruthardt

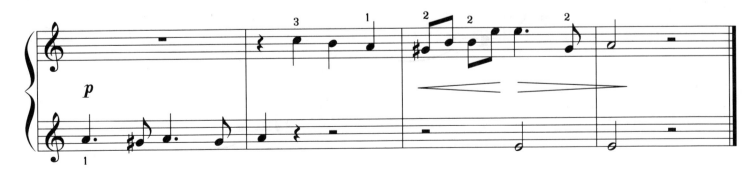

Technique

Inverting a triad a second way.

1. Practice playing from first inversion to second inversion as you did on page 29.

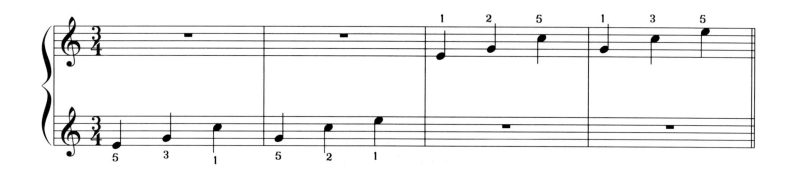

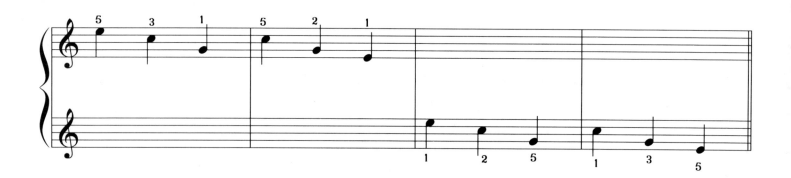

Practice the F and G triads like this.

When you can play them with your eyes shut, you really know them!

2. Practice second inversion arpeggios with C, F, and G triads.

Another Scale to Practice
Play F scale the way you played C scale on page 17.

WP318

UNIT 6

A New Way To Count

Challenge

To count one beat for each eighth note.

To Get Ready

1. Study these explanations of time signatures:

   3 tells you to count three beats in each measure
   4 tells you to count one beat for each quarter note

   6 tells you to count six beats in each measure
   8 tells you to count one beat for each eighth note

2. Writing the counting between the staffs in these examples.

3. Practice counting aloud to six, accenting beats 1 and 4.

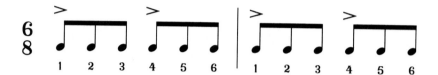

That is how $\frac{6}{8}$ feels!

4. Write the accent marks in Example A.

Something is missing in Example B! Make the example correct. (If you need a reminder, see page 3.)

When an eighth note gets one beat, it changes the way we count all the other kinds of notes.

5. Color the boxes, using one color for each note. Write the correct number in the blanks.

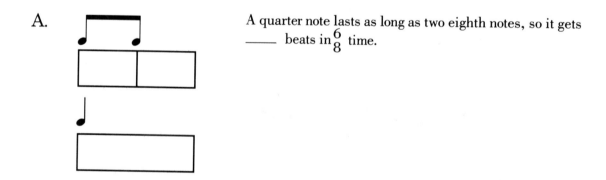

A.

A quarter note lasts as long as two eighth notes, so it gets _____ beats in $\frac{6}{8}$ time.

WP318

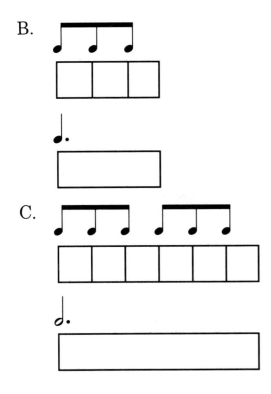

B.

The dotted quarter note lasts as long as three eighth notes, so it gets _____ beats.
(The quarter note gets _____ beats, and the dot gets half of that, so the dot gets _____ beat.)

C.

The dotted half note lasts as long as six eighth notes, so it gets _____ beats.
(The half note lasts as long as four eighth notes, so it gets _____ beats. The dot gets half of that so the dot gets _____ beats.)

There are no whole notes in $\frac{6}{8}$ time. Why?

6. Write the counting below the notes in the following exercises. Then clap, tap, or play rhythm sticks while counting aloud.

42

7. Write the correct time signature in each box.

A.

B.

C.

D.

E.

F.

WP318

$\frac{6}{8}$ **time changes the way we count rests.**

8. Fill in the blanks in the following examples.

   ❼ is the same as _____ (kind of note), so it gets _____ beat.

   𝄽 is the same as _____, so it gets _____ beats.

   𝄽· is the same as _____, so it gets _____ beats.

   𝄽 ❼ together get _____ beats.

   ▬ lasts through the whole measure, so it gets _____ beats.

Color the boxes for the notes. Leave the boxes for the rests uncolored. Write the counting under the notes.

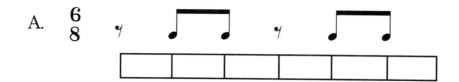

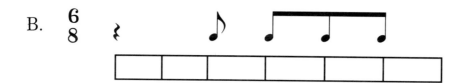

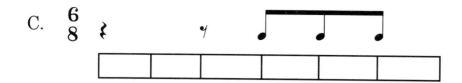

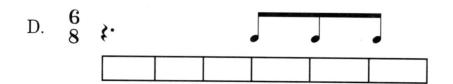

WP318

9. Write the counting below notes and rests.
   Play each exercise on any key with any finger.

A. — B. — C. — D. — E.

F. — G. — H.

46

Technique

Pedaling Correctly in 6/8 Time

Challenge

To "change" the pedal when needed.

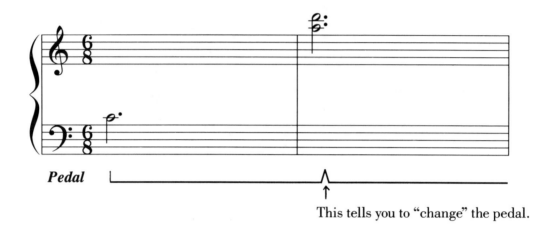

This tells you to "change" the pedal.

To change the pedal does not mean to use a different pedal. It means to let the pedal up and then put it back down again while you hold the keys down. Use the ball of your foot to move the pedal.

To Get Ready

Your teacher will help you learn these exercises.

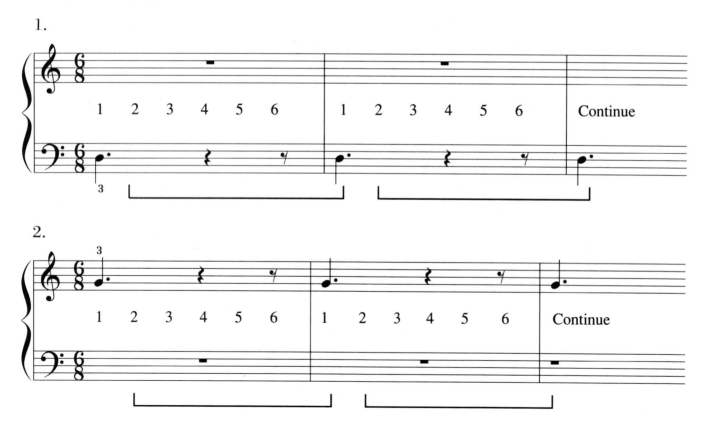

WP318

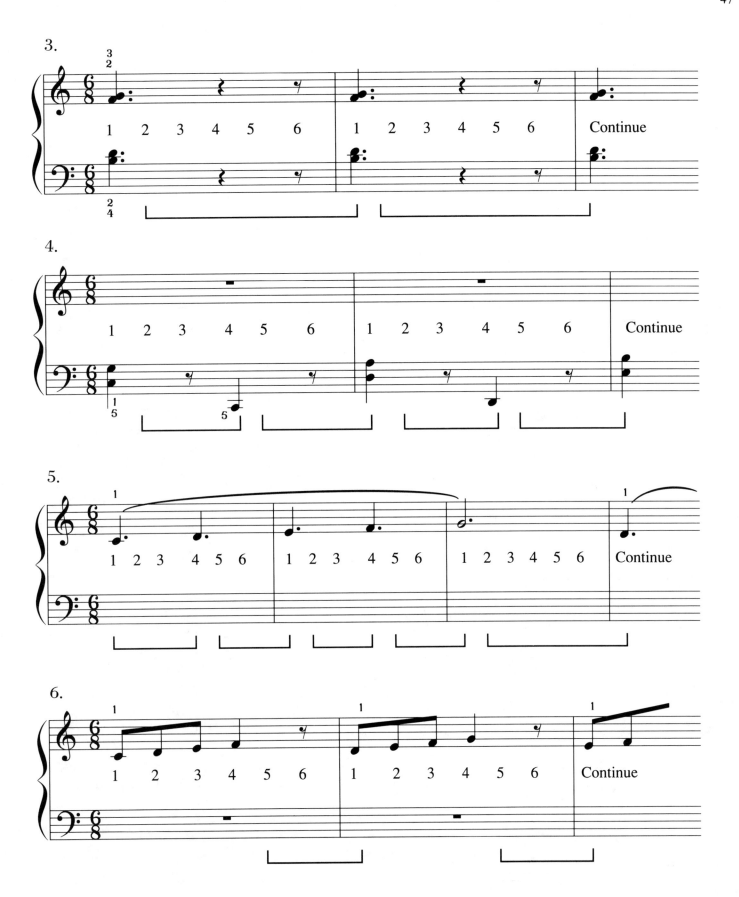

THE GONG WOKE ME UP BUT I WENT BACK TO SLEEP

I WATCHED THE SUN SETTING

I WAS WONDERING...

SKIPPETY-HOP

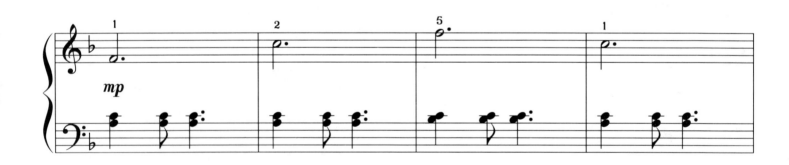

FEELING GREAT!

A tempo tells you to return to the regular tempo after a *ritardando*.

MY LUCKY DAY

GITTY-UP

WP318